BORN TO HAVE JOY

8 Steps to Living the Life of a Gypset

LYKKE STJERNSWÄRD

To claim your 4 free bonuses, please visit:

www.borntohavejoy.com

Published by

10-10-10 Publishing

1-9225 Leslie St.

Richmondhill, ON

L4B 3H6

Canada

Printed in the United States of America.

ISBN: 978-1-927677-64-3

ACKNOWLEDGMENTS

This book is dedicated to you. Dear precious travel friend,

I am writing to honour a family legacy

Dear family of humanity,

Forever loving and grateful for

your love, support and inspiration

TABLE OF CONTENTS

FOREWORD

Born To Have Joy by Lykke Stjernswärd is intended to help you understand that you can achieve more success and happiness in your life if you explore your uniquely personal values and not compromise. The values of relationship, caring and doing the right thing are needed in both family and business today, and the author would argue that without them, business is looking at an inescapable downfall. This book will encourage you to allow yourself to challenge your beliefs, find your values, guide your life accordingly and learn to be yourself. By being truthful to yourself and others, you will find huge power and success. In this book:

- You will develop your personal branding
- You will explore the interlinking cycle of beliefs, values, actions and outcomes that reinforce each other
- You will see that as you hone your skill at being authentic, you will start to become more powerful and that power feeds and supports your beliefs.

Raymond Aaron
NY Times Best Selling Author

INTRODUCTION

The legacy of my first name and surname has had an impact on who I am.

Lykke Stjernswärd translates to 'Lucky Star Sword' or 'Happy Star Sword'.

Therefore, I have chosen to live up to my name and to be a lucky dreamer and explorer.

In this book, I share anecdotes from my life as a lucky, happy dreamer.

As a little girl, at bedtime, my mother used to pray for me in Swedish as follows:

...lyckan kommer,

Lyckan går,

Den Gud älskar,

Lyckan får.

I used to think that 'lyckan' and 'Lykke' were the same and that my mother was referring to me when she prayed.

The prayer translates to:

…happiness goes away,

Happiness comes,

The one who loves God,

Will find happiness (lyckan / Lykke)

With this prayer, my loving mother set the first foundation to my faith, even if I stayed rather confused for many years. I wondered why anyone who loved God would get... lyckan / Lykke (happiness). I was not sure why anyone would get me, but I thought, let's see what happens when the moment presents itself.

I was too shy to ask my mother why that would be, but I did fall asleep peacefully.

A caring art director I used to work with, Mr. Leslie Jessop, showed me a book called The Family of Man created by Edward Steichen for the Museum of Modern Art, New York. When I wished to make a career move, we walked out of the office and sat down on a bench not far from St Paul's cathedral in a smallish green park in the heart of the city of London. Leslie brought up the book and asked me, 'What would you like to be doing in five years' time?' His question was a big question for me. I thought that the answer needed to be as big with a purpose which fit the size of the question.

That is the moment the idea crossed my mind: 'Wow, could one have a job where one could just focus on taking picture of families in the world such as Edward Steichen had assembled in his book?' Maybe one day I would also be a photographer taking pictures of families and relationships.

As a departure present from work, Leslie gave me a five-year diary in which I wrote daily for three years, just five lines per day. It was after writing for three years that I discovered that life is lived in patterns, and some feelings like fear, joy, restlessness or happiness, for example, come back on a regular basis.

Vogue Milan offered me a job as a graphic designer when I graduated from the Art College of Design Europe. I was flattered but chose not to join and went to practice in London instead. But I remember telling myself that if I ever worked for Vogue, I would come back as a photographer. I have been fortunate to get an assignment for Vogue Nippon since.

It was when working in Kiev in Ukraine for six months that I developed a friendship with my camera. To be an expat young woman in Kiev, I took my camera with me whenever I went sightseeing. Like that I could stop and connect to the new culture that I was discovering.

A friend of mine suggested to me for fun that I should write about my life as a photographer, and another friend admitted that she likes to live vicariously through me. This book will not be about my life as an artist. This book is about mindfulness and my way of showing gratitude for what I have learned so far. By sharing my modest insights, I wish you to take this knowledge for yourself and build on it further. Why not write to me? I would like to hear from you. - contact@lykke.ch

CHAPTER 1

Joy Is to Experience Life

To experience life. At birth, did you get your one-way ticket to life? You must have if you are reading this book. I am very aware that I did get my ticket and since then I have been undergoing a transformational process. No air miles to collect with this ticket. My best prescription to experience life is to live it with passion and to enjoy every day as a gift. Love in the present and live for the future.

Personally, I believe I was born into a family where there were a lot of expectations regarding my birth. I was given the name Lykke, which is a beautiful Danish first name that means 'felicity' and 'joy'. I was born after the premature death of an eleven-month-old baby boy in a family that already had two sisters.

I was born to be joy after grief.

After grief in my own life, I made a conscious decision that I was born again to live my destiny as a woman. Professionally, I have grown the brand FémininSacré™; it has been a great opportunity to give a voice to my cherished feminine nature. I would also like to pay a tribute to my sisters, mother, grandmothers, goddaughter and the next generation of girls and women. FémininSacré™ is a brand of jewelry and charms meant to forge ties and connect hearts. The mission of my brand is to empower you to live with trust and coach you in self-development to attract what you desire into your life. Why work with us? We share with you positive vibes so you can see yourself as the extraordinary, beautiful woman you truly are and for you to enjoy your potential at 100%: confident, trusting, intuitive, rooted and a change-maker.

'Select the keys to access your energy centers.'

The seven chakras

Chakras govern all aspects of the individual: physical, emotional and spiritual. When balanced and functioning properly, optimal health is achieved. Belief in the chakras is thousand of years old and comes from Hinduism. Throughout the book, you will come across sentences written to address the seven different chakras. You will select the message that appeals to you. You could also select from our collection of holistic bracelets to experience the power of daily awareness.

Mindset addressing the chakra, the energy center, called the Crown:

Confident, I access my infinite resources.

Your lucky charm bracelet: *En confiance, j'accède à mes ressources infinies.* - femininsacre.net

As an entrepreneur, I am also establishing the brand '8value'.

We engage in growing leadership, powered by the 8value network.

We offer to visualize your values to empower you to be a 100% change-maker.

We guarantee an infinite amount of positive value for you through self-development and good personal branding. Invest with us in the capital of trust plus life experiences. 8value stands for:

1. you are the center

2. mobility

3. network

4. anticipation

5. trust

6. visibility

7. joy

8. vitality

Your lucky charm bracelet: _An investment in knowledge always pays the best interest._ Benjamin Franklin (femininsacre.net)

To be aware of my luck in life gives me the desire to live and share my luck joyfully.

On a weekday, I walked the streets in London. I was walking on my favourite street, Regent's Street. I like its architecture and the beautiful curve the street as seen from Picadilly Circus. When looking into the Aquascutum shop window, my photographer's eye fell onto a poster. More than full size, there was a man holding a camera, dressed in a raincoat, smiling at the passingcrowd where I was. He was gorgeous and passionate in taking photos. He was real as far as he was printed onto an advertising poster. I thought to myself: *Where can I meet a man like that?*

What is the probability in a lifetime that the man on the poster that you desire to meet moves into your home? I would not be able to calculate that probability. But what I know for a fact today is that the model on the poster did move in with me and my flatmate. The Argentinian model on the poster called three weeks later after I saw the poster of him, asking for a room that was available to rent in the flat we were living in.

I almost forgot about my Canadian flatmate's wedding the same day the model came to check out the room. He introduced himself , showing his portfolio of modeling work, and the third picture he showed me was him on the poster in the Aquascutum shop. The poster was moving in with us!

The model, Nicolas Malleville, has since become a friend. I admire him; not only is he good looking, but he eventually realised his dream to open up a hotel to host his friends and family. It is called CoquiCoqui Residences Yucatan in Mexico.

Born to have joy. Dear Mother Earth, thank you for having me over as a guest. I would like to live in your 'home,' respecting your resources and contributing to your sustainability.

Born to have. And born to be. Find the right balance for you between having and being. Beautiful souls have a secret. They have compassion, live trust and have joy for life.

Your lucky charm bracelet: I believe in creating, I lead with my heart. - femininsacre.net

'Let there be light' (Genesis 1:3), which, translated into Latin is 'Fiat Lux.'

'Post Tenebras Lux' (the motto on the flag of the city of Geneva).

Translated as 'Light after darkness.'

'Fiat Lux.'-'Let there be light'
(Genesis 1:3)

When working as a photographer, it is soothing to work in the present and to capture the beauty of light. Soul searching and art photography have in common that you are given an image of your state of mind in a given context and time frame.

Let the light of your being live, it's your beauty. Your glow may be the key to success in your life.

A life is filled with stories. How do you story-tell with photography? For inspiration, I recommended a photography book of great poetry: *The Essential*, by Duane Michaels.

Joy. I have many sources of joy.

My driver for joy in the past: my child and teenage joy and confidence were built on living the unique moments as a member of a united family. My vital joy as a young adult woman was to be in love. My joy experienced with my siblings was to be part of the same family. My professional joy was to learn from inspiring mentors.

My driver for joy in the present is to experience joy in my life in the here and now. It is important to use my inner resources for my own life, to take my destiny into my own hands.

My driver for joy for the future is to facilitate the creative process, influence and joy, encouraging you/me to design your own mood-board to attract what you desire into your life. The power of your thoughts can influence how events turn out. Visualize your objectives, your dreams and your perfect lifestyle. Attract those desires into your life.

On a daily basis:

Take five minutes to reflect on what your sources of joy are.

I had to decide what to do before I die. I was very impressed when reading a book written by a nurse who wrote about her experiences in accompanying terminally ill patients. Her conclusion was that we should all learn how to die. Once you accept death as the ultimate end, then you plan to live your life fully. The book is called: *'Learning to Die: Knowing I will Die Someday, How then Will I live?'* by Dr. Judith Rich

I have had a life game plan since I was sixteen.

My life game plan:

1. Be a photographer
2. Fly to the moon
3. Live by the waterfront
4. Be a scholar
5. Be a mentor
6. Be a philanthropist
7. Be a parent
8. Be part of a family business
9. Marry my best friend
10. Live in a united family
11. Leave a legacy behind me

Your life game plan:

Dream up a plan and print an action plan for yourself.

The following book had a great positive impact on me: *The Purpose Driven Life*, by Rick Warren. This book helped me shape my strong purpose in life.

Another book which has had a great impact on me is *The Seven Habits of Highly Effective People*, by Stephen R. Covey

Enlightening reading: *Siddhartha*, by Hermann Hesse

One way to think of life is that 'It's just a ride' in the spirit of the highly inspiring singer Lou Doillon. It's always a good time to listen to her song 'Devil or Angel'.

It's just a ride.

Life is all just a journey. Every journey starts with a scream. Every discovery awakens curiosity. Schedule time with yourself. Make learning a priority.

On a daily basis:

With the help of the wonderful app Shazam, I can list the music which accompanies my drives. These are some of the titles picked up on the road which triggered joy when I was driving. Hope you can enjoy them as well on your ride: **Loca** -Shakira / **Video Games** - Lana del Ray / **Bullets** -Tunng / **I Gotta Feeling** - The Black Eyed Peas / **We Found Love** -Rihanna Teat and Calvin Harris / **Femme QueJ'aime** - Jean-Luc Lahaye / **Who's Thinking About You Now?** - Jason Mraz / **Kiss and Say Goodbye** - The Manhattans / **Get Lucky** - Daft Punk Feat. Pharrell Williams / **Ho Hey** - The Lumineers / **Wavin' Flag** -K'naan / **Blurred Lines** - Robin Thicke Feat. T.I. & Pharell / **Reality** - Richard Sanderson.

CHAPTER 2

How To Be A Gypset

'Gypset (Gypsy + Jet Set) are an emerging group of artists, musicians, fashion designers, surfers, and bon-vivants who lead semi-nomadic, unconventional lives.'
Source: www.facebook.com/pages/Gypset

'Julia Chaplin, founder of the often-imitated but never duplicated Gypset style and author of *Gypset Travel* has set her style on the map of the world.'

August, 2013 on Facebook: 'aloha Lykke! Love Nico, Francesca and Tulum. So happy you are enjoying Gypset. happy travels xx Julia'

Vanity Fair's Elissa Schappell chose *Gypset Travel* as one of her "Essential Bohemian Books."

'Julia Chaplin also curates very special sales for members only. It is a style guide of boho interio items, jewelry and sarongs.'

'Yuppies, Yippies, Jet Setters, Bright Young Things, Generation X, Generation Y . . . and now the Gypset. Fusing the ease and carefree lifestyle of a gypsy with the sophistication of the jet set, the Gypsetters are artists, surfers, designers, and bon vivants who live and work around the globe, from Jose Ignacio, Uruguay and Ibiza, Spain, to Montauk, New York. *Gypset Style* explores the unconventional, wanderlust lives of these high-low cultural nomads and the bohemian enclaves they inhabit, as well as their counterculture forbears, such as the Victorian explorers, the Lost Generation, the Beatniks, and the hippies. And along the way, author Julia Chaplin looks back at quintessential gypsy boho moments in social history.' Source: *Gypset Style* by Julia Chaplin on amazon.com

Stand out from the ocean of sameness.

Stand out. I admire you a lot. I like you. You are the one. Be you. Be in-credible.

Your words count for something. Your vision is important to the world you live in. You are born to have joy. You are a shining star. You have the right to be happy.

Your lucky charm bracelet: *Reach for the moon, even if you miss, you'll land among the stars.* – Les Brown (femininsacre.net)

Ocean of sameness. Love nature. The ocean inspires a lot of respect.

Stand out from the ocean of sameness. Dare to be you. Do contribute to a better world by being a change-maker. Innovate. Develop your talent. With enough practice, your talent is what you do best.

On a daily basis:

To be is to live here and now.

Your lucky charm bracelet: *Être, c'est vivre ici et maintenant.* - femininsacre.net

'Gypsetters are artists, surfers, designers and bon-vivants who live and work around the globe.' Gypset Style by Julia Chaplin

Be together in vibrating locations.

Be together. *Unite in a spirit of pure freedom.* Share and team up.

Invite members to share with you the little things in life that makes a difference.

These could be your values, your yoga classes, your routines, or your most loved food recipes. Or to snooze under a tree in late afternoon on a summer day.

Be visible with people you love. Hang out with people who inspire you.

Free yourself from envious and controlling personalities.

Love recipe, cooking for two:

- Boil 1 cup red lentils in 3 cups of water
- Add 1cs salt
- ½ can of coconut milk
- 1 cs green curry
- 12 frozen shrimp
- Serve with mango chutney

Vibrating locations. *The road less travelled.*

The coolest places around the network, by the people who know them best.

My favorite place to meet Gypsets is in Mexico on the beach at CoquiCoqui Tulum. My friend Nicolas Malleville and his wife Francesca Bonato have built their dream there. - coquicoquiperfumes.com

Inspiration from my favorite corners-of-the-world beaches and hotels:

- In Australia, in Perth, meet up on Cottesloe Beach.
- In Australia, in Sydney, meet up on Bondi beach for surfing.
- In Bali, stay at the Begawan Giri in Ubud. - begawan-giri.com
- In Brazil, in Trancoso, meet up on the square by the church.

- In Brazil, in Rio, meet up on Praia de Ipanemaand relax by the pool at Fasano. - fasano.com.br
- In Brazil, in Sao Sebastiao, meet up on Praia das Calhetas.
- In Egypt, the AdrereAmellalSiwa Oasis. -adrereamellal.net
- In France, in St-Tropez, meet up at Club 55. Check out the boutique there for boho-style beachwear.
- In Mexico, in Sayulita, meet up on the beach for some yoga lessons.
- In Mexico, in Compeche, The Hacienda Uayamon. - haciendauayamon.com
- In Nepal, in Katmandu, meet up for the Shiva festival.
- In Sicily, in Mazara del Vallo, meet up on the beach in Granitola for kite surfing. Visit Granitola, the lighthouse on the edge of the world. If you need windsurfing gear, Albino Burgio's Sea Store Sicily will help you.
- In South Africa, in Cape Town, meet up in Camps Bay and stay at Hotel. - 12apostleshotel.com
- In Sweden, in Falsterbo, meet up for seaside walks to see migrating birds.
- In Spain, in Ibiza, visit the hippy market: lasdalias.es

Engage, invest and exchange values.

Engage. The most thrilling way to enjoy life is to be the better part of yourself. In the spirit of a shared economy, unite and exchange values. For the first time in history, we live in a world of overcapacity. Find the capacity and exchange value.

Improve the world distribution of capacity and contribute to social and environmental change. Become a change-maker in your field of expertise. As an entrepreneur, you find the opportunity and understand your marketplace. Leaders know how to serve the customer, work with employees and inspire them. The companies who will survive in today's economy are the ones who create change; they are not just profit oriented, but also find a way to give back to society.

Invest. *Make money by doing what you love.*

Find hideouts with the perfect vibe. Innovate. Align your thoughts, words, energies and actions. Set up a restaurant of your choice, build a boutique hotel on the beach, set up a Gypset fashion shop, teach yoga as you travel, cook beautiful ayurvedic food for your friends. Invest your energy and your time where you love making a difference.

Exchange values.

Find capacity and improve global capacity by sharing know-how.

Be Free. Be Flag. For more 'Flag Stories,' visit: flag.lu

On a daily basis:

You are the change-maker.

I am now about to reveal the bonus of chapter two.

- **Use Lise-Lotte's and Nancie's bonuses**
- Setting goals and achieving them is a vital part of success. I invite you to meet two entrepreneurs.
- By special arrangement, I have permission to allow you, my dear reader, to collect a surprise gift when you present yourself in their shop with this book *Born to Have Joy*

Lise-Lotte Nydahl, founder of Nydhal Interior in Skanör, Triangeln 2, Sweden.

Nancie Wohlers, founder of Boutique Duo sur Canapé in Geneva, 10 rue Verdaine, Switzerland.

On a daily basis:

Align your thoughts, words, energies and actions.

CHAPTER 3

Accept The Pain To Die Every Day A Little And To Wake Up The Next Day

Every day. Transformational process.

Each day, I choose three reasons to express my gratitude.

Your lucky charm bracelet: *Chaque jour, je choisis 3 raisons pour exprimer ma gratitude.* - femininsacre.net

It requires a trust in life to really dare, and we all have different levels of basic trust in us.

Mindset addressing the chakra, the energy center, called the Third Eye:

Calming my mind to follow my intuition.

Your lucky charm bracelet: *Eteindre mon mental, pour suivre mon intuition.* - femininsacre.net

Respect you and create you.

Respect you. Keep a healthy balance between the needs of your body, mind and spirit. As the Chinese say, we have two brains: one in our head and one is in our guts. Follow your intuition. You can read your feelings in your body. My belief to keep a healthy spirit is to keep in mind the equilibrium formed by the number three, for example: the Father, the Son and the Holy Spirit / a father, a mother and a child /me, my mentor and my Pilates teacher. Recognize where to set limits for yourself and with others for your own well-being. If your vital space is not respected, create space for yourself. This requires energy and one should not be afraid to say no. Give yourself the chance to empower yourself. It is also easier to have respect for others when you respect yourself. Empower relationships to empower trust. Empower parents to empower children. Empower siblings to empower each other.

Mindset addressing the chakra, the energy center, called the Heart:

The cure for fear is love.

Your lucky charm bracelet: *L'antidode de la peur, c'est l'amour.* - femininsacre.net

Create you. Start up the transformational work to create your brand and to create visibility for yourself. Use your inner resources to build your own life.

As a photographer, I cast light onto my model and empower my clients to empower themselves. In a photo session, I make my client feel that she or he is the center of attention; I shine light onto them, I encourage them to be on stage. They are the actors of their lives. When my models find their glow, they can illuminate their personal life path.

On regular intervals:

See your life in the palm of your hand.

Needed for this test: 1pen and 1 sheet of A4 white paper

- On an A4 piece of paper, draw the outline of your right or left hand. It's not important which hand you choose to draw. What is important is to get the outline.

- On your drawing, within the outline of your palm, write at the bottom center of your palm the state of mind or how you would like to feel about yourself.

- Select the five most important projects in your life which would allow you to feel as you have chosen. Write down those 5 selected projects in each one of the finger outlines. The order in which you write down your projects is not important.

- One of those 5 projects will change more often than you can control without changing how you feel about yourself. Point out one of those 5 projects.

- Now you have an overview of your life. You can clearly see which 5 projects you need to run in parallel in your life to live well with yourself.

- The one project you selected that could change more often is the area you are ready to compromise with. This is a good thing to know. You know that you have to compromise and you know where to make concessions.

This is a very powerful tool to have an overview of what is important to you in your life. Look at the visual sample below:

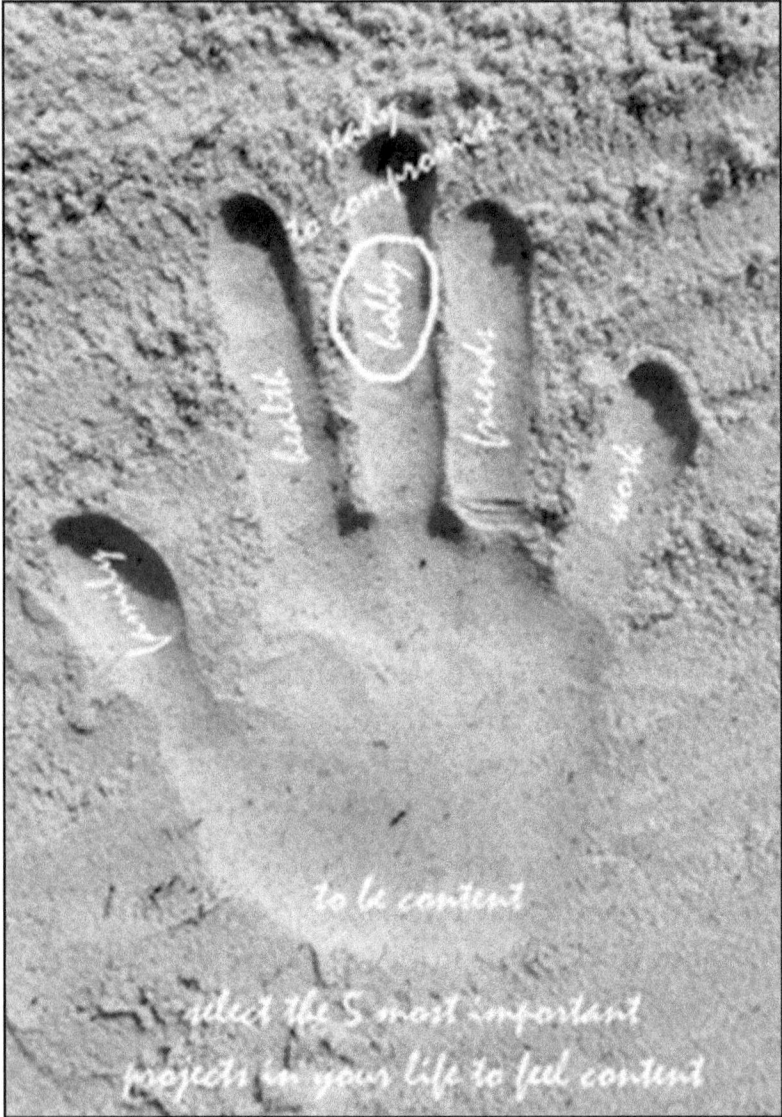

Define a personal value for each essential moment in life.

Personal value. Set healthy limits between yourself and others.

Accept that death is inevitable and decide what you want to do before you die. Develop your winning attitude to life, choose gratitude as your best friend, unite the young at heart with partners you can work with, create fun, invest in trust, respect vital momentum, take responsibility, spontaneously serve your clients and the market, practice tolerance, respect others, get informed, get involved, practice transparency (truthfulness), give birth, innovate, invest in new technologies.

All emotions have names. Name each emotion for what it is. Unmet needs trigger negative emotions; met needs trigger positive emotions.

A beloved and liberating read: *Non-violent Communication* by Marshall Rosenberg

At 8value.com, we will be happy to help you visualize your values and design promotional items accordingly. Our company values are mobility, network, anticipation, trust, visibility, joy, vitality and you. Every journey starts with a small step.

Beyond stories.

Live life free and beyond stories. Free yourself from the stories that put you down. Laugh and dance on the beach. Meet with DoñaEsra in Corfu in summer if you have not met with her before in Berlin, India, Mexico or Istanbul. She has channeled her incredible beautiful energy into her life plan. She calls herself a dreamer.

'DoñaEsra's workshops, called 'Power Journeys', are tools to help you become the fullest expression of yourself and to overcome the limitations that hold you back from creating the life that your free soul will manifest. Her stories allow you to understand yourself better and become a wonderful reflection, assistance and inspiration for the real workshop of your own daily life. Doña Esra's energy is always encouraging and empowering, wherever you may be on your personal journey. Her strong love, clear questioning and gentle guidance will hold you in a well balanced place while your old skin is being easily shed and your new one is appearing fresh, smooth and bright. Let her words take you on a journey beyond your mind's constructed limitations and make deep change and transformation possible.' Source: toltecwisdom.eu

Mindset addressing the chakra, the energy center, called the Throat:

Healing my wounds by liberating my words.

Your lucky charm bracelet: *Soigner mes maux, libérer mes mots.*- femininsacre.net

Mindset addressing the chakra, the energy center, called the Solar Plexus:

I give back to others what belongs to them.

Je rends aux autres ce qui leur appartient. - femininsacre.net

Essential moments in life. Every life starts with one big scream. Every journey starts with one small step. Every discovery awakens curiosity. Every encounter starts with a smile. Passion butterflies are expressions of happy travels and happy encounters.

Settle down to become the tree of your life. One sunny summer day, I hugged a tree in my garden and compared myself to the tree. I admitted to the tree that it was doing a better job than me of being a tree. I chose the tree to be my best guide for self-development. The tree was not questioning its nature, was not doubting its reason to exist; the tree was rooted, the tree was growing year after year, the tree was firm and strong, the tree has branches reaching out. The branches are lush with leaves, the branches are welcoming to birds, the birds can rest and nest on the branches. A tree is not a dragonfly; a tree is not a migrating bird. A tree stretches for the sun, and the sun is a source of life for the tree. The tree lives its legacy between its roots and its branches. A tree can be part of a group of trees, a tree stands next to other trees, a tree is not clingy. Trees can be of different natures and still leave space for each other to grow side by side. Weather conditions can shake a tree, but if the tree is flexible it will not break. A tree is an inspiring guide and a best friend.

Select the keys to access your energy centers.

You will select the message that appeals to you. You could also select from our collection, one of our holistic bracelets to wear it around the wrist, to experience the power of daily awareness.

Mindset addressing the chakra, the energy center, called the Root:

To succeed, I care for my roots.

Your lucky charm bracelet: *Pour réussir mon envol, je soigne mes racines.* - femininsacre.net

Become a celebrity. Welcome yourself daily in front of the mirror with a smile.

Smile and be famous for yourself. Be your own groupie and best friend.

By being genuine, you become credible and increase your celebrity status.

'Creating has saved me from despair and traveling has given me the feeling of living several lives.'
~Isabel Allende

The early bird catches the worm.

Affirm your personality. Si bon d'être soi. So good to be oneself (home). To know who you are is the key to success. You cannot change time, but time can change you. Anticipate life and invite time to work on your side and with you.

On a daily basis:

Live trust.

'Creativity has given me a goal and a voice.
I feel connected to many spirits in the world
and to my soul.' ~Isabel Allende

CHAPTER 4

Spot The Opportunities For Joy

Spot the Opportunities. *The spirit of joy.* We live in a world of opportunities. We can unite with great flair. Invest in something new. Contribute to gross national happiness.

The vision of joy. To unite brains and hearts in the present for a bright future. We have a contract between generations to honour. Visualize your values and create a team spirit that can help people reach objectives together. Together, we can all contribute our visions for development and innovation.

This is my personal prescription for a positive mindset:

Each day, I choose three reasons to express my gratitude.

Feel joy to live here and now. I love in the present. I live for the future.

Joy. I was introduced to Trea Tijmens, founder of SuccessMatch, seven years ago. I have had the privilege to work as a photographer since the beginning of her business. SuccessMatch is a Geneva-based dating agency that focuses on introducing international working professionals who are looking for a partner to share their good life with. It is a fantastic experience to meet clients in such an important transformational moment in their life. I have felt deep joy every time I have been involved in a photo session. To cast light onto the model, to see the person with my heart and empathy, letting the client experience being the center of attention, to connect with a human being one to one in a confidential moment, has been most enriching for me and contributed to high job satisfaction. To build a relationship based on trust for the moment of the photo session, to witness a smile in the model's eyes and to see confidence expressed with body language has brought me moments of joy. Contributing as a photographer is very much working in the present. The decisions are made here and now. To be happily engaged in the present is my experience of joy.

Here and now.

To be is to live here and now.

Your lucky charm bracelet: *Être, c'est vivre ici et maintenant.* - femininsacre.net

As a photographer, I have chosen to be in a position of a storyteller. I have observed the world around me and focused on capturing images of nurturing, loving relationships. It has been bliss to channel my vision on this selected theme. The flow of positive vibes exchanged between me and my models is elevating.

Experience a caring photo session for respecting your individual worth and seeing your personal glow. One photo session is a transformational experience and worth a thousand words.

On daily basis:

Life is lived in the present.

> *'Unite in a spirit of pure freedom, fusing*
> *the ease and carefree lifestyle of a gypsy with*
> *the sophistication of the jet set.'*
> Gypset Travel by Julia Chaplin

Dear to my heart are the following points: the importance of forging ties, connecting one to one, seeing with the heart, engaging in the present, to live with trust, to bond here and now, to reach a common purpose together as a team, unite in pure spirit of freedom and find hideouts with the perfect vibe.

Experience joy in the small things that matter.

The experience of joy. Invest in something new. Anticipate a return on fun.

Mindset addressing the chakra, the energy center, called the Sacrum:

The orgasm of life is joy.

Your lucky charm bracelet: *L'orgasme de la vie, c'est la joie.* - femininsacre.net

Even if the use of the word 'orgasm' makes some people blush, in this context for me it is a perfect use to express the intensity of joy needed to love life.

Small things that matter. We have a contract between generations to honour.

A fresh glass of water; how tasty is that? A hug; how comforting is that? A look in the eyes; how bonding is that? A firm handshake; how trusting is that? A smile; how friendly is that? An invitation; how genuine is that?

70% of communication is expressed with our body language. Therefore, we can speak many languages.

On a daily basis:

Contribute to the gross national happiness as much as you contribute to the gross national product.

100 goals achieved by my clients.

8value.com Branding you. Our design network is all about growing leadership and forging ties among skilled professionals. By building relationships of ***trust*** and anticipating innovative solutions, we work with you for a bright future, empowering you to be **100% change-maker** by creating **visibility** for your values, the foundation of your successful business. We visualize your values with your help. Your values are your keys to deliver **vitality** to your business, **joy** and great experience to your customers.

Testimonials. My customers are inspiring role models for me.

'I have been working with Lykke for over eight years now and highly recommend her as a photographer. She is able to make our professional clientele enjoy their photo shoots and consistently delivers high quality work. Well done, Lykke!'

-Trea Tijmens, hearthunter; professional matchmaker and dating coach, link'in singles for love. Founder of SuccessMatch.ch & DatingSuccess.ch

'Lykke is a very qualified photographer with a special focus on people. She is very detail oriented and has excellent people skills. She ensures a relaxed atmosphere during photography sessions.'

-Patrick Ashworth, Founder and CEO at Shopping4Fans.com

'By the dynamism, the inventiveness and her foresight in

everyday life, both in the choice of her company's products and in partnership, Lykke demonstrates a mastery of skills as an outstanding business and creative head. Also, her optimism and spontaneity offer any collaboration a taste of common adventure and joy in all the products that she knows how to innovate and highlight.'

-Raoul Gross, writer of sacred texts and messages for FémininSacré™

'So great to see you at Giving Women. I bought one of your bracelets and it is love. I am wearing it with the one from Design Days. They make me so happy!!! You are such an amazing artist. See you soon.'

-Joan Flanagan, your New York friend who you think is Swedish

'I'm interested to take part in the "shining beauty and mind" contest organized by Dukas copy ("Miss Dukas copy 2013"). Dukas copy is a forex trading bank, headquartered in Geneva, owned by a Russian businessman Andrey Duka (hence the name), and successfully operating internationally. I want to check with you that it's fine if I use the photo shoot pictures for the contest.'

-Ivetta Gerasimchuk

'After photographing my yoga teacher, who impresses with her skills, she wrote back when looking at her photos: "Isn't this beautiful? You are an artist. I am proud of you."

-Melinda Spitzer, *yoga teacher*

Brainstorming session to pin down values that matter: awakening, intuition, fun spirit.

-Fabien Jakob

On a daily basis:

Men have a great role to play to empower women.

Women have a great role to play to give support to men.

I am now about to reveal the bonus of chapter four.

- Use FémininSacré's bonus
- Setting goals and achieving them is a vital part of success. I invite you to share your inspirational quote to have joy.
- By special arrangement, I have permission to allow you, my dear reader, to own a charm bracelet by FémininSacré for free and you can get it by registering simply by going to the website, borntohavejoy.com

CHAPTER 5

Host Joy And Vitality In You

Vitality

Strength and consistency, I love and do what pleases me.

Force et constance, j'aime et fais ce qui me plaît. –Raoul Gross, Dr. Phil. (femininsacre.net)

Transparency is the key to open a new chapter in mutual trust.

Lack of trust is what creates sadness in life. Lack of trust robs you of your vitality. Your life is your human right.

Living in the present young at heart.

Living in the present.

Experience the power of daily awareness.

To live happily, I have learned the long way that one has to live happily in the present and enjoy the present. Living in the present happily builds the future of tomorrow.

Young at heart.

Love my inner child, keep my child lightness.

Your lucky charm bracelet: *Aimer mon âme d'enfant, garder ma légèreté d'enfant. –Raoul Gross, Dr. Phil.* (femininsacre.net)

'Find hideouts with the perfect vibe.'

Invite a bright future, start-up and empower.

Bright future. Anticipate. Loving in the present. Living for the future.

'Invest your energy and your time where you love making a difference.'

Start-up. Action plan. Business plan.

I invest my energy in the positive present moment.

J'investis mon énérgie dans le positif moment présent. - femininsacre.net

Empower. 'Empowering women to empower women.' - givingwomen.ch

'Get Involved. Get Informed.' - endignorance.org

'100% change-maker.' - 8value.com

On a daily basis:

Invite colours into your life. The most impressive colour guide expert that I have come across is Japanese author Shigenobu Koybayashi. He has written the following books: Color Image Scale and Colorist. I like his books.

Grab the momentum which is vital for you.

If you love the life you live, you will live a life of love.

Grab the momentum.

Life is lived in the present.

Vital for you. Protect your vitality. Know your human right to exist.

Stay pure at heart. The truth will set you free.

Select the keys to access your energy centers.

You will select the message that appeals to you. You could also select from our collection, one of our holistic bracelets to wear it around the wrist, to experience the power of daily awareness.

Mindset addressing the chakra, the energy center, called the Throat:

Healing my wounds by liberating my words.

Your lucky charm bracelet: *Soigner mes maux, libérer mes mots.*- feminsacre.net

The mindset addressing the chakra, the energy center, called the Solar Plexus:

I give back to others what belongs to them.

Your lucky charm bracelet: *Je rends aux autres ce qui leur appartient.*- feminsacre.net

49

CHAPTER 6

Trust: Access Your Infinite Resources

Trust. *Live with confidence.*

Mindset addressing the chakra, the energy center, called **the Crown**:

Confident, I access my infinite resources.

Your lucky charm bracelet: *En confiance, j'accède à mes ressources infinies.* - femininsacre.net

I love in the present. I live for the future. The past has designed who I am today.

There is not one truth in life. Truth is relative to a given context with given protagonists.

Tree of life.

A tree is an inspiring guide and a best friend of mine.

There is no room for envy nor jealousy in my heart. If those feelings come to me, I quickly listen to those feelings as friends who warn me to adapt or let go.

If something is important to me, I will stand up for it.

Know where you come from.

Mindset addressing the chakra, the energy center, called the Root:

To succeed, I care for my roots.

Your lucky charm bracelet: *Pour réussir mon envol, je soigne mes racines.* - femininsacre.net

On a daily basis:

To succeed, understand the context you live in and take into account all the stakeholders.

> '*Gypset is an emerging group of artists who lead semi-nomadic, unconventional lives.*'
> - Gypset Travel by Julia Chaplin

Find your personal challenger

Your challenger. Your emotions are your personal challenger. Emotions are friends who have a name. Each emotion called by its name is recognized for its pure nature. Life is so much easier when you call emotions by their name. Creativity and writing can help to express emotions. Therapy can also be a way to be acquainted with the name of emotions and their secondary effects. Trust your intuition and handle your emotions; they are great milestones.

Mindset addressing the chakra, the energy center, called the Third Eye:

Calming my mind to follow my intuition.

Your lucky charm bracelet: *Eteindre mon mental, pour suivre mon intuition.*- femininsacre.net

Your intuition and standards are your best allies.

Respect your needs and believe in your dreams and you will be your own personal challenger.

We come naked to the world. We can build and get what we want in life.

We can lose it all. Then we just need to start again. It is in adversity that character shows. Talent is skills practiced with perseverance and hard work.

We view the world through our own personal filters.

Photography has given me the chance to show what I see with love and compassion. Developing the brand FémininSacré™ has given me a voice. I feel connected with my sisters of humanity.

I am happy to have been published in *The New York Times* and *The Herald Tribune* with a portrait of Mr. Bernard Piguet, chief auctioneer at the Hôtel de Ventes, Geneva.

'I think the memory of those we have loved and lost is with us. I do not see any ghosts, but I see spirits all around me, and the love of departed beings, they helped me on

55

many occasions. *Writing also saved me from despair and gave me the feeling of living many lives. This gave me a purpose and a voice. I feel through writing connected to millions readers and connected to my soul.'*

- Isabel Allende

Create new opportunities

To create. You have this life to create. Creativity is given to all, but it is recognized by only a few.

Something new. Live your life's game plan.

I like challenges through sport. Consider the health risks before participating.

Paragliding in Verbier

Bungee jumping in Belmont

Walking around the Matterhorn over the glaciers from Italy to Switzerland

Trekking in Nepal

Heli-skiing on le petit Combin in Valais

On a daily basis:

Positive thinking is the greatest untapped natural resource in the world.

CHAPTER 7

Embrace Quality Time

Embrace life.

Mindset addressing the chakra, the energy center, called the Third Eye:

Calming my mind to follow my intuition.

Your lucky charm bracelet: *Eteindre mon mental, pour suivre mon intuition.* - femininsacre.net

Live your life's game plan.

Attract what you desire into your life.

Your life game plan. Dream. Innovate. Create. Focus. Decide. Change. Make it happen. Believe. Trust. Go for it. Anticipate. Vitality. Joy. Mobility. Take responsibility.

Your power of attraction. Positive thinking is the greatest untapped natural resource in the world. Positive vibes, nurturing and creative energies. The creative power, influence and joy.

On a daily basis:

Write your own travelogue.

8 Steps of Living the Life of a Gypset.

1. Gypsy + jet set: emerging group of artists, musicians, fashion designers

2. Bon-vivants who work and live around the globe

3. Lead semi-nomadic, unconventional lives

4. Fusing the ease lifestyle of a gypsy with the sophistication of the jet-set

5. Bohemian style

6. Gypset travel + Gypset style by Julia Chaplin

7. Explores the unconventional wanderlust lives of high-low cultural nomads

8. Happy travels

'Every discovery awakens curiosity.'

Draw your life line: Make a drawing of your lifeline as you see it. Ask your best friend to do a drawing for her or his life. Compare the drawings and see how different a lifeline can be. It is a surprising learning curve.

Invite love into your life.

Invite love. Your body is your temple. Experience the power of daily awareness. Start the day with a salutation to the sun or / and include you and your loved ones in your morning prayers. God loves you.

The most precious gift I received when breaking up with my fiancée was a prayer from his mother. She wrote: 'I pray for both of you.' At the time, I did not understand how someone could sit calmly and just pray instead of acting on the situation. What struck me is that she wrote 'for both of you.' Her prayer created such an impact on me that I signed up for three years of Bible studies to find out how someone can sit calmly and just pray for you when you are in distress and feel that it can be one of the most supportive way of loving. Her compassion extended further than just for her son. That was a great life lesson. I am forever loving and grateful for her prayer.

Your life. Optimal health. Chakras govern all aspects of the individual: physical emotional and spiritual. When balanced and functioning properly, optimal health is achieved. We share with you positive vibes for you to see yourself as the extraordinary, beautiful person you truly are, for you to enjoy your potential at 100%. Love is the way.

'Chakras govern all aspects of the individual: physical emotional and spiritual.
When balanced and functioning properly,
optimal health is achieved.'

The 'secret keys' to access your energy centers. Presenting our selection of holistic bracelets, carriers of positive messages, designed with charms of luck, love and protection.

1. To succeed, I care for my roots

2. The orgasm of life is joy
3. I give back to others what belongs to them
4. The cure for fear is love
5. Healing my wounds by liberating my words
6. Calming my mind to follow my intuition
7. Confident, I access my infinite resources
8. To be is to live here and now

We love forging ties with unique gifts. Visit our website: femininsacre.net.

We warmly welcome new distributors around the world. Please contact us for further information.

Accept loving invitations only.

My lovely yoga teacher, Melinda Spitzer, will invite you to love, to care for your body's agility, to breathe, to let go, to open up. You will now find her teaching in Zürich.

Last but not least, you will meet my lovely Pilates teacher, Fanny Lechot, in Geneva. Her body is her work of art. When she teaches Pilates, she can show every subtle movement of a muscle. I realized with her that my brain is not the only muscle in my body. - pilatescocoon.com

*'The most thrilling way to enjoy life
is to be the best part of yourself.'*

I am now about to reveal the bonus of chapter seven.

- Use 8value's bonus

- Setting goals and achieving them is a vital part of success. I invite you to share your values to have joy.

- By special arrangement, I have permission to allow you, my dear reader, to own a change maker bracelet by 8value for free and you can get it by registering simply by going to the website, borntohavejoy.com

CHAPTER 8

Indulge In Vital Moments

Vital moments

Schedule time with yourself.

I like the number three. Life is biology. Life is energy. Life is spirit of innovation.

Why invest your energy in at least five essential projects in your life?

Can you visualize a chair with four legs? If the chair loses one leg, the chair can still stand up on three legs. So if one project fails in your first four choices, you will still be able to stand up.

Find the area in your life where you are ready to compromise without losing out on your vitality.

Select the keys to access your energy centers. Chakras govern all aspects of the individual: physical, emotional and spiritual. When balanced and functioning properly, optimal health is achieved. Belief in the chakras is thousands of years old and comes from Hinduism. I would not make the mistake to present myself as a specialist on Hinduism. I invite you to do your own research on the subject.

Elaborate a winning attitude in life.

Winning. You are born a winner.

Life in five words: What. An. Incredible. Wonderful. Experience.

Words are silver and silence is gold. Learn to say yes. Learn to say no.

Last but not least:...for you to see yourself as the extraordinary, beautiful person you truly are for you to enjoy your potential at 100%. Love is all.

Attitude. Creative power, influence and joy. My perception for a winning attitude in life is to believe in intelligent design, which is something mightier than myself. 'God loves me' are some of the most impactful words I've ever heard, followed by 'I will pray for you both.' The qualities that I find the most relevant and which make me smile are: gratitude, joy, love, to be, to have, content, mindfulness, humility, respect, strength, consistency, awareness, to love and do what you love, thrift, perseverance, equilibrium, forgive but do not forget, invest in knowledge.

*'Positive thinking is the greatest untapped
natural resource in the world.'*

Take responsibility for your thoughts and actions.

Take responsibility. I was not lucky. I deserved it.

Your thoughts. Build dialogue. Grow for autonomy.

If you love the life you live, you will live the life you love.

Your actions. Have a beautiful quality to you. Be open, cool, sophisticated and have a purpose.

On a daily basis:

As a photographer, when photographing relationships, my eyes are in my heart. I observe with my heart. So much beauty is seen with the heart.

Be a change-maker.

The spirit of a change-maker. What is your vision for innovative change? How will you connect and forge ties? Visualize your values.

On a daily basis:

Get paid to do what you love.

I am now about to reveal the bonus of chapter eight.

- **Use Aaron's bonus**
- Setting goals and achieving them is a vital part of success. My mentor and friend Raymond Aaron has written a bestselling hardcover book Double Your Income Doing What You Love. He is recognized as the world's number one authority

on goal achievement. In fact, on the back cover, there are testimonials from giant celebrities who use his program. One such testimonial is by Jack Canfield, the co-creator of the Chicken Soup For The Soul series of books. Here is his testimonial: 'The reason I personally chose to use this amazing system for myself and for my company is that, bluntly stated, it is the most powerful system ever created.'

By special arrangement, I have permission to allow you, my dear reader, to own a copy of Mr. Aaron's book for free and you can get it by instant download simply by going to his website, aaron.com

CHAPTER 9

Be Creative And Laugh A Lot

To create is gathering essential things of life.

Fun in life. Fun-raising as in fundraising. Look out for a return on fun. Invest in fun. Making a lasting difference to education in peoples lives. Contribute to change for good by donating to givingwomen.ch or any foundation of your choice. Engage at an early age in a cause that is close to your heart. You will feel part of something bigger then yourself. You can choose to donate financially or your time and skills.

So love builds.

Your lucky charm bracelet: *Só o amor constrói.* -comitepelavida.org

Strength and consistency. I love and do what pleases me.

Your lucky charm bracelet: *Force et constance, j'aime est fait ce qui me plaît.* - Raoul Gross, Dr. Phil. (femininsacre.net)

Cities generate creativity, mobility and freedom. For your own creativity, find the city or place that inspires you. Creativity is in our DNA. To be alive, we have been created. Choose your own project to create and realize yourself. You have the power for creativity, influence and joy.

Here, I would like to refer to a book called *Urban Safari.2*, by Bobo Karlsson.

'He writes about twelve big cities. In 2010, the World Mayor Prize was given to Marcelo Ebrard in Mexico City. Berlin's mayor, Klaus Wowereit, attracted a lot of youth to his city with the mantra 'Penniless and Sexy'. Collaboration between business life and communities create opportunities. Chicago's mayor, Rahm Emanuel, through cooperation between local government and industry, wants youth not only to stand with a degree in hand when they leave school, but also work experience.' Source: Sydsvenskan Nyheter

Humanity and good technology apply to law enforcement.

Life is a sparkling mix of challenging values that push almost relentlessly create new designs, to generate new ideas and provoke new thoughts.

Follow your intuition.

Your intuition.

Mindset addressing the chakra, the energy center, called the Third Eye:

Calming my mind to follow my intuition.

Your lucky charm bracelet: *Eteindre mon mental, pour suivre mon intuition.* - femininsacre.net

On a daily basis:

Intuition never lies. It is your personal radar. When you are connected to a source of unconditional love for you, you can live by trusting your intuition.

'Be in-credible.'

Develop a spiritual path

Spiritual. The potential of unlimited mindfulness.

A small contribution may be sufficient to accomplish great things.

The fundamental desire of goodness equal happiness

Set limits.

'The wisdom of an artist.'

'A Toltec is an artist of life.'

'The word *Toltec* has its origin in Mexico and comes from the Nahuatl, an old Aztec language, and means *artist*.'

'Toltec wisdom is the wisdom to consider life as art: You

are the artist, and art is your life. Everything you do. Not only your deep passions. Your job. Your relationships. Your private time and your hobbies. The whole day, every moment, every action–your entire life is an expression of yourself, a piece of art. You have the freedom to create your life how you want it to be no matter what religion you choose to live or what nationality or culture you belong to.'

- 'Respect always comes first in the wisdom of the artist:
- Respect for your own art.
- Respect for the art of others.
- Respect for your decision to change your art if you do not like it anymore.'

Source: toltecspirit.com

'Live trust.'

To live trust. Building healthy relationships based on trust. Trust life.

On a daily basis:

I invest my energy in the positive present moment.

CHAPTER 10

Invite Joy Into Your Secret Garden

My secret garden. That little place in my heart, a place I had forgotten to spend time in. That is how secret my personal garden was to me. Become the caretaker of your own equilibrium.

A wonderful place to connect with your secret garden is to visit:

Insens – at the heart of the senses – a haven of peace in the heart of the city of Geneva. Meet with Ata for yoga.

Book a transformational treatment of Tulamassage & Tulayoga , a unique type of bodywork developed by Louka Leppard. Heal your Self through caring for your body - the foundation and container of your well-being. - insens.ch

Live with passion here and now.

Live with passion. I am filled with gratitude for my luck in life. Life has been very generous and therefore I have lots of anecdotes to share.

Late in life, I did sign up for Bible studies when my heart was bewildered. There I met ladies who introduced themselves as 'caterpillars'. I thought it was rather amusing that they were referring to the specific moment in their faith as caterpillars, and I was looking forward to see us all transform into butterflies. It was not as poetic as that.

When the ladies referred to themselves as caterpillars, it was the company name their husbands were working for.

Your lucky charm bracelet: *Vivre avec passion ici et maintenant.* - femininsacre.net

Here and now. This book is on living now. The only life we have is now. It is in the present that you shape your future. As you choose to be creative and laugh in life, you are the designer of your own life game plan.

On a daily basis:

Quiet the negative and the positive will manifest.

'Born to have joy.'

Host events and join the party.

Host events. Invite people into your life.

'What I learned is that we do not need to follow our thoughts. We can meet our feelings in our body instead.' –Björn Lindeblad, Swedish Buddhist Monk.

Listen to his guided meditations on spotify: https://play. spotify.com/album/1OshCeN7bOVldh83rvufSP

Join the party. Link the world for a worthy cause. Create new opportunities for yourself.

On a daily basis:

Laugh and dance.

> *'You have the right to be happy.'*
> *-DoñaEsra*

Laugh and dance on the beach.

Meet on the beach. Laugh and dance on the beach. In Corfu in August, meet with DoñaEsra if you have not met with her before in Berlin, India, Mexico or Istanbul. I see her as a magnificent wild mustang who has channeled her incredible beautiful energy into her life plan. She calls herself a dreamer. DoñaEsra runs a workshop called 'Power Journeys'. She teaches the Four Toltec Wisdoms. Her master is Don Ruiz Miguel.

'The Four Agreements are:

1. **Be Impeccable with your word:** Speak with integrity. Say only what you mean. Avoid using the word to speak against yourself or to gossip about others. Use the power of your word in the direction of truth and love.

2. **Don't Take Anything Personally:** Nothing others do is because of you. What others say and do is a projection of their own reality, their own dream. When you are immune to the

opinions and actions of others, you won't be the victim of needless suffering.

3. **Don't Make Assumptions:** Find the courage to ask questions and to express what you really want. Communicate with others as clearly as you can to avoid misunderstandings, sadness and drama. With just this one agreement, you can completely transform your life.

4. **Always Do Your Best:** Your best is going to change from moment to moment; it will be different when you are healthy as opposed to sick. Under any circumstance, simply do your best and you will avoid self-judgment, self-abuse and regret.' Source: toltecspirit.com

On a daily basis:

If you value the life you live, you will live a life of value. - 8value.com

www.ingramcontent.com/pod-product-compliance
Lightning Source LLC
Chambersburg PA
CBHW060553100426
42742CB00013B/2547